Anaya Bruno

Gentle Guide To Religious Freedom

With A Focus On Unlearning Harmful
Christian Teachings

The products and the book are not associated with any product or vendor mentioned in this book. None of the companies referenced within the book have endorsed the book.

First edition
ISBN 978-0-99-157289-2
Typesetting by G & D Enterprises Inc

DEDICATION

For myself, who had the courage to
deconstruct on my own

&

For my father, who always validated
my feelings and made my ideas feel
extraordinary

Disclaimer!

This guide is not intended to replace proper therapy and should not be used to self-diagnose mental illness.

This guide is meant to provide guidance and support to people who may be affected by religious trauma, negative church experiences, and/or Scrupulosity OCD.

If you think that you may be struggling with mental illness, I highly suggest that you contact a mental health professional.

This guide is focused primarily on the religion of Christianity, but its suggestions can be applied to any religion.

Contents

FOREWORD

When Linda Creed and Michael Masser wrote the words: "I believe that the children are our future, teach them well and let them lead the way, show them all the beauty they possess inside; give them a sense of pride to make it easier, let the children's laughter remind us how we used to be", they were speaking to me.

My daughter, Anaya Bruno, certainly possesses the skills required to shine a light on the future. Ana, as I refer to her, has a mind of gold and in her vision, she sees a world which can be made better by our collective contributions. Ana is compassionate and purposeful, and this book speaks to her selfless passion.

Gentle Guide to Religious Freedom is only one of Ana's ways of communicating with her peers and the world. In this book, she offers kind ideas which – if understood in the spirit with which they are meant – could make a difference in someone's life and experiences.

Have a read and share your sentiments. This is what Ana would want from this project.

It is my honor to extend this book, which is partly dedicated to me, to you. I, therefore, present Anaya Bruno to you. Please receive her work and welcome her to your world.

-Alex Bruno

Personal Testimony

Religious deconstruction is a sort of taboo subject. This may be due to the fact that for many people, religion is a part of culture and tradition. It may also provide feelings of comfort and hope to people facing trials in life. However, for many others – including myself – except for being a source of comfort, religion has been a facilitator of anxiety and mind-control, leading to decreased mental wellbeing. Many aspects of religion that encourage fear, submissiveness, extreme humility, and forced admiration poison people's minds and alter their mental functions. Unfortunately, I was one of those people.

From an early age, I was exposed to many Christian teachings, some of which were harmful to me. I lived my life in extreme vigilance and fear of evil and wrongdoing. I felt obliged to worship the "right" way and for a sufficient amount of time. But no matter how much I did so, I still felt worthless. I was taught to not trust myself in fear that evil forces controlled the minds of people who did not completely "submit to God's perfect Word," which I was convinced was the Bible. I found myself feeling inherently sinful and dirty, contributing to my beliefs that I needed to depend on something other than myself to feel even the tiniest bit of worth, or else I would be deserving of nothing but eternal torture.

In the back of my mind, many of these teachings seemed extreme and even illogical to me, but I suppressed my gifted, analytical mind in fear of what might happen if I wasn't humbly submissive to these teachings. My father always encouraged me to not keep myself contained in a box and to think outside of it. However, the fear-rooted teachings were too far entangled into my mind, causing me to reject his wise guidance because I was convinced that what I believed was right and that nothing else possibly could be. I convinced myself that I believed these things out of genuine love and admiration of God, but the truth is that I never got the chance to think for myself and figure out what I truly believed.

This wasn't "spiritual discipline" that I was experiencing, I was experiencing symptoms of mental illness.

Relearning One's Worth

    A fundamental teaching of Christianity is that one is inherently worthless. As young children, many people have attended Church services in which the pastor may have preached about the doctrine of Original Sin. Put simply, this Doctrine basically teaches that people are inherently evil and deserving of eternal punishment. But in an attempt to make up for this teaching, the pastor may have preached the doctrine of Christ's Atonement, in which God sacrificed His one and only Son in order to pay for the wrongdoings of man.

    These kinds of teachings are usually sold with the slogan that "this is the most perfect example of love," but to young children, these teachings establish the idea that people must be ashamed of themselves unless they submit to the teachings of a religion. Christian Doctrine also says that salvation is a "free gift," but then claims that a person must submit to God and accept Jesus as their Lord and Savior in order to be saved from the Hell that they deserve.

Children who internalize these teachings may grow up to have distorted views on love and how loving relationships should function. They may believe that it's okay to be highly-dependent on others and to believe that they're nothing without them. They may believe that it is just for loving parental/guardian figures to hold threats of punishment above their heads in order to gain respect and praise, instead of simply forgiving them of their mishaps without a cost.

Although these teachings may seem innocent on the surface, they morph children's minds to think in ways that excuse harsh and abusive behavior. These teachings convince children from early ages that respect is equivalent to fear. It is preached over and over again that it is good to have a "healthy fear" of God. However, this statement is clearly an oxymoron because fear of a person is not healthy. Instead of raising children who feel comfortable enough to speak up for themselves and to decipher respectable figures from hurtful ones, this teaching raises submissive and insecure children who obey not out of respect, but out of pure fear of the alternative. This isn't love. This isn't healthy. Nothing about these teachings scream "free gift" or "good news." And to make matters worse, children at early ages don't yet have the ability to think critically for themselves.

They don't have a choice to decide if they truly believe in these teachings. They don't have a choice to step back and think "this may not be right." Instead, they are spoon fed threatening teachings and are forced to humbly submit to them in order to avert eternal damnation.

These internalized feelings could contribute to emotional and mental issues as children grow up. If this story seems familiar to you, I hope that the following list allows you to feel some comfort and to unlearn some of these harmful teachings:

***

1. *You are not inherently sinful.*

Out of all of the eggs in your mothers womb, *you* were chosen to experience life. You are an extension of the universe itself. You have the ability to do wonderful things and have wonderful ideas. You are not broken. You are perfectly imperfect. Every flaw that you have is an essential part of your whole being. You can make mistakes without having to feel crippling shame and the strong desire to "repent" or pay for all of your wrongdoings. You deserve forgiveness because your heart is pure. You don't need to be made perfect by anything or anyone because you already are. And you have the right to refuse the "sinful" label without feeling arrogant.

2. *You are worthy of love and acceptance.*

You are worthy of love and acceptance the way you are. Nothing about you needs to be "fixed" because you're already whole. You are worthy of compassion despite your past mistakes, your present insecurities, and your future slip-ups – which you're bound to make.

3. *You are not going to Hell.*

For the course of human history, the concept of eternal damnation has been portrayed and explained in many religions and myths. These stories have been used to teach people and to instill fear into them in an attempt to make them submit to certain beliefs. However, there are lots of religious and spiritual teachings/practices in the world. All over the world people are born, die, and experience life in their own ways. Supposed spiritual encounters with past loved ones have been claimed by some people and alternative explanations of the afterlife have been conveyed by others. And honestly, no one is sure of what happens after death. However, I hope that you find some peace in knowing that nothing is forever, and there is truly no such thing as "nothing." Just as this life is a phase, so is death. And there was no way of guessing that you'd enter this earth before you did, so who knows what may come after – whether it's like this life or not. And things don't really turn into nothing, they only transform into something else. So in the midst of uncertainty, I hope that you can try to accept the idea that nobody is certain of how life after death will be – not even the people who recorded their beliefs in the Bible (which consists of retold versions of first-hand, has been translated multiple times throughout the course of history, has been heavily influenced by many factors overtime, and likely contains parables and myths that are possibly taken in incorrect context or too literally).

***

Here are some reflection questions to
meditate on:

1. *Which harmful beliefs have I internalized
   from religious teachings?*
2. *How have they negatively affected me?*
3. *What can I replace these beliefs with?
   What do I truly believe?*

Detachment From Purity Culture

Teachings of purity culture have been practiced for centuries, and they tie a woman's worth to her virginity and overall "purity" of sexual activity. A couple of common teachings in this culture are those of premarital abstinence and modest dressing. It is typically deemed unjust for people to engage in premarital sex in Christianity, which contributes to a sense of shame regarding people's free practice of sexual activity. However, the focus of purity has always been on women because it is believed that a woman losing her virginity is analogous to a flower becoming crippled.

According to traditional Christian teachings, the stoning and shaming of women due to their lack of sexual purity was deemed just according to God's Word. People who internalize these teachings view sex in a taboo light and may not receive proper sex health education. It may also prompt many people, particularly women, to become ashamed and viewed as "devil-spawns" for living in a way that isn't seen as righteous according to the teachings of the Bible.

Traditional Christian teachings also put a large amount of pressure on women to dress in ways that won't cause men to fall into "sexual impurity." This kind of mindset is similar to the one in which the blame of rape and/or sexual assault is typically placed on women for "asking for it," except for holding men accountable for their pervetous behavior. These teachings are not only extreme, but they are sexist and support harmful patriarchal ideals.

If any of these experiences resonate with you, hopefully the following reassurance will bring you some peace:

***

1. You are more than your virginity.

Whether you've engaged in premarital sex or not, your worth isn't tainted. You have the right to feel pleasure freely without feeling sinful or less than those who do wait until after marriage.

2. Sex isn't a taboo or evil thing.

Sex is a natural thing that almost everybody experiences in their lifetime. Sex wasn't made for marriage. That is an outdated and partially sexist societal view. Sex is for reproduction, affection, expression, and pleasure. You deserve the right to experiment sexually before marriage if you'd like to.

***

Here are some reflection questions to meditate on:

1. *Has purity culture personally affected me? In what ways?*
2. *Do I feel comfortable around the topic of sex?*
3. *How can I take mindful action towards overcoming sexual shame?*

Freedom of Sexuality Expression

It can be heard over and over again that "marriage is between a man and a woman." Similarly to common teachings of purity culture, this mindset is an outdated one and it supports homophobic ideals. It also relates to the outdated belief that a woman's worth is attached to a man, hence once a woman marries a man, she is seen as his. This is evident by females historically adopting males' last names in marriage. However, as time moves on and we develop more progressive attitudes towards women's worth and how familial setups should be, we also need to become more accepting of homosexuality.

Homosexuality isn't an unnatural thing – although it is often claimed to be. In fact, homosexuality is present in many species of animals, proving that such behavior isn't artificial. Sadly, due to loving the people that they love, many members of the LGBTQIA+ have been taught by many churches that they're either deserving of Hell or destined to go there because of their sexuality. This is extremely unfair and doesn't reflect the image of a loving and accepting God.

We as a society need to move forward and become more accepting of people as they are. Despite your personal views on homosexuality, your beliefs shouldn't discriminate against homosexual people and/or their rights to be themselves. If you've been hurt by homophobic teachings, such as the aforementioned ones, I hope that the reassurances listed below provide you with some comfort:

***

1. *Love has no boundaries.*

You can't choose to love or be attracted to a certain sex and/or gender. Your love isn't unnatural. Not only is it natural, but it is beautiful and worthy of acceptance. A loving God wouldn't punish you for loving the way you naturally love.

2. *Homophobia isn't just.*

Any culture that justifies homophobia is harmful. Under no circumstances should homophobia be seen as a righteous or honorable thing to practice. Any god who would order for their followers to be homophobic isn't worthy of worship.

***

Here are some reflection questions to meditate on:

1. *Have Christian teachings affected your mental wellbeing as a member of the LGBTQIA+? In what ways?*
2. *Do you feel supported by supposedly "loving" Christians as a member of the LGBTQIA?*
3. *In what ways can you unlearn harmful Christian teachings surrounding be homosexual.*

Welcoming Discomfort

In Christianity, it is taught that we should not trust ourselves, but shall only rely on the understanding of God. (You may refer to my three deconstruction writings at the end of this book if you'd like to hear more about my perspective on this doctrine.) However, I encourage you to be yourself and to let your mind wander and discover new things. Question old, dogmatic, and problematic philosophies in order to move towards more positive and helpful ones.

Teaching young children that they should fear themselves and that self-pride is a symptom of evil influence may cause them to grow up to be insecure about themselves, their ideas, and their worth. These teachings stunt intellectual growth and perpetuate fear instead of creativity, which could be considered traumatic. We need to encourage the youth to think for themselves, to say no to dogmatic principles, and to refuse to follow teachings that don't align with their personal morals.

Below, I've listed some questions to prompt critical thinking. Engage with them and embrace the discomfort that you feel because it means that you're resisting the anxiety surrounding stepping out of your comfort zone.

***

1. *Why do you believe that your understanding of events is the only right way?*

2. *Do you truly believe that the Christian image of God is an image that depicts love? Would you like a romantic partner to function the way the Christian God does?*

3. *Do you truly love God, or do you fear him?*

4. *If you could say one thing to the Christian God without punishment, what would you truly say?*

Stop Tying Mysticism & Superstition Into Everything

The following chapter is directed to those who decide to leave their faith and does not need to be followed if one decides to remain in their faith

Have you ever stared at the sunset and said that "this is proof that my understanding of God is real"? Have you ever witnessed a miracle and immediately became convinced that it was due to your religious practices? If so, I encourage you to think critically with me.

Many occasions and/or experiences may raise feelings of awe and euphoria in people as a product of biological processes. Witnessing a childbirth, singing with a crowd of people, and running in the rain produces positive feelings that may be attributed to mystic phenomena. However, I want you to think about this. If, according to a belief system, pencils are the product of bees, and pencils exist in the world, does that mean that the bees caused the pencils' existence? And if someone were to believe that "the Christmas spirit" is a result of Santa Claus, does that mean feelings of warmth during Christmas time is valid proof of Santa's existence?

When people don't quite understand the logic behind things, they tend to fill in the blanks with theories and myths. Some of these stories have been widely accepted. However, it doesn't mean that they are necessarily the truth. You can feel happy when singing a worship song with others without that happiness coming from "the Holy Spirit." And when people pressure others to pray to their god because "He has answered their prayers," I want you to think about all of the unanswered prayers. You may be thinking *"Why the pessimism? Shouldn't you focus on the positive?"*, but hear me out for a second.

When Christianity claims that God provides for all who love Him and ask humbly of Him, and one faithful person is forsaken by dying of hunger or disease, this claim is immediately disproven. It is misleading because it asks for submission and admiration in exchange for provision – which doesn't seem very graceful to me; And it deceives people by giving them a false confidence that they will surely get what they need. Not to mention that many prayers in Jesus' name have failed to be answered, while other kinds of prayers – which technically shouldn't work according to some Christian teachings – have been.

This goes to prove that lots of the supposed "proof" that churches and Christians claim to have about their beliefs being the only truth may just be a result of people filling in the blanks where they don't have a sure understanding.

Find Your Own Purpose

Many traditional Christian teachings surround "following God's will" and having humility in your personal desires. In fact, humility is typically hyper-emphasized in Christianity. It is frequently taught that trying to find your own path is a symptom of pride and that you must rely on God's predetermined will for your life in order to act righteously. However, this raises feelings of impending doom because the sad reality is that lots of unfortunate and devastating things happen in the world.

People get sick, people lose everything, and people die. And by believing that everything is predetermined for you, a sense of pessimism may arise knowing that the God that allowed for these terrible things to happen "according to His will" has total control of your life. *If these bad things could happen to others, who says it couldn't happen to me?*

If you've had thoughts similar to this one, I have good news for you. What if I said that you had a choice? There are obviously situations in life that are out of your control. But you can find some hope in knowing that the decisions that you make in life can alter your fate. Nothing is completely set in stone, and you have the power to control certain things in your life without feeling unrighteous. If you have a dream that you desire to follow, you have the right to make it happen.

Stop tying your identity to religion and enslaving yourself to something you don't even understand. Instead, take action and control the things that you are able to.

Stop People-Pleasing

As aforementioned, Christianity provides hyper-emphasis on humility. It is taught that those who are humble now will reap glory later. However, these teachings are sometimes taken to the extreme, and there is a sense of shame surrounding self-pride.

Traditional Christian teachings justify the submission of wives to husbands and slaves to masters, reflecting a humility-focused ideal. Although an important virtue in some circumstances, by internalizing that having pride in yourself is wrong, people may struggle with low self-esteem, pessimism, and fear of assertiveness.

These conditions are harmful and shouldn't be encouraged. Instead, you should find pride in yourself and what you stand for because your ideas are worthy of respect. You should have the confidence to disagree with and even refuse to abide by harmful teachings and/or advice – even if they are from a position of authority – in order to stay true to your morals.

If you find yourself people-pleasing and lacking assertiveness as a result of internalizing these harmful teachings, I encourage you to find some respect for yourself. Self-respect does not necessarily mean that your opinion is better than others. It just means that your opinion matters too.

Stop "Sin-Checking"

Christianity can evoke intense feelings of anxiety due to hyper-vigilance of wrongdoing. Christian teachings perpetuate fearful atmospheres surrounding moral failure and "sinning."

Frightening doctrines, such as the one of Original Sin, thrive off of the shaming of people for engaging in behavior deemed morally unjust in the eyes of God. There is also an emphasis on repentance and striving for moral perfection at all times – or at least pretty close to it. This createsblack-and-white thinking by encouraging people to see things in polar extremes such as *"Any time that I lie, I've sinned"* and *"If I'm not perfect, I'm a sinner."* Extreme black-and-white thinking may prompt people to engage in obsessive and compulsive behaviors in an attempt to neutralize the intense anxiety that comes from being over-consumed with one's moral righteousness. For instance, someone may have used a white-lie at work by claiming that there was traffic in order to excuse their late arrival. However, by being given strict instructions on how a righteous person should live, said hypothetical person may overanalyze the intention of their behavior and may engage in frequent repentance and/or "soul searching" rituals. Such behavior is not only extremely time-consuming, but it is unhealthy, stressful, and can become debilitating if not managed properly.

If you struggle with "sin-checking," I want to reassure you that you are a good person, because "bad people" do not care about their morality. You know your heart and intentions more than anyone, and there is no one constantly monitoring them and holding you accountable for every mishap. You are allowed to make mistakes and learn from them without having to experience the debilitating anxiety of constant "sin-checking."

Welcoming Diversity of Thought

Although Christians claim to be humble, too many of them are arrogant in their beliefs because they believe that they have the only true answer, and that others are deceived or led by Satan himself. However, the truth is that no one knows everything, and that there are many sides to the truth. No one deserves to feel like their beliefs and viewpoints are less than and that they deserve punishment for diversity of thought.

If you take anything from this guide, I hope that you remember that your ideas, experiences, and viewpoints are valid and worthy of respect.

Final Words

I, unfortunately, had to discover the deconstruction process and engage in it on my own. And I must say that it was one of the loneliest and scariest things that I've ever done and ever hope to do. I've built my whole personality, up until last year, upon religion, and I've lived in fear of discovering myself. I had to go through mental torment every single day, most days until the point of tears, because of Christian teachings, and I was a slave to my Scrupulosity OCD.

I didn't feel like I could fully tell anyone about this experience because most of my family are Christians, and I was afraid that they would probably excuse and/or support it. However, if I had one person to thank during this whole journey, it would be my dad. He has never made me feel ashamed of my emotions, he always makes me feel seen and heard, and he is literally a male adult version of me. I see a lot of my personality traits in him, so I feel like he is with me wherever I go. I would definitely say that I'm a daddy's girl because although he might not always agree with them, he never shames me for having out-of-the-box ideas and he always sees merit in my views, whether he agrees or not. He is considerate, affectionate, and patient. And although I didn't truly get to experience the "loving father" figure in religion, I got to experience the best version of it with him.

However, I know that many people aren't as lucky as I was to have someone to support them during this debilitating journey. So I decided to write this guide, because if I can save one person from going where I went,

I would feel accomplished in life. So I hope that you move forward with courage and pride because you deserve freedom. This guide is meant to be the voice for all who feel silenced by religious hurt. May our collective pain and questions be heard.

If you decide to religiously deconstruct and need inspiration in your journey, I suggest that you read the analytical writings that have made this guide possible. They were written before I decided to make this book, and it's really impactful seeing how much my thoughts and ideas have changed since. They were inspired by general knowledge that I have accumulated over the years and my experiences of being a Christian.

Religion... To Save or To Be Saved From?

Growing up in a strictly religious household could adversely affect a child's wellbeing, far into their adulthood. The characteristics of certain religions, such as Fundamentalist Christianity, promote self-depreciation, toxic prideful attitudes, divisiveness, constant anxiety, and hence feelings of overwhelming depression. It is taught in Fundamentalist Christianity that one is inherently sinful and worthless alone.

It is believed that only through a savior figure dying a brutal death that us human beings, as such messed up creatures, could potentially be saved from the death that we supposedly brought to ourselves. Such a story is backed up by the Adam and Eve myth, which claims that the first woman, Eve, tempted Adam to eat an apple from a forbidden tree, which caused sin to enter the world. However, this fable has been long outdated with a plethora of scientific evidence overwhelmingly supporting evolution. This is a point that I want to elaborate on.

A lot of history's religions have been based on superstition and mysticism. Lots of phenomena that were previously believed to have Divine origin were later suggested otherwise by science. In fact, religion has been used to justify a lot of inhumane things such as genocide, war, and murder. And even weirder, these things have been justified in the name of God.

This "God", according to the Bible, is the most perfect example of love, suggesting that we should follow in His guidance. But the question I pose for Christian apologetics is this: *If the Bible is the truth of God, and God killed all of these people in the Old Testament, and he is the same now and forever, should we murder?* People promote the narrative that God's ways are above our human understanding to justify such contradictory messages of the Bible. But if that logic is true, then how can you trust what you claim to certainly know about God? If you can't understand why He'd make promises and not keep them, how do you know for sure that He is good? Is that not your interpretation of scripture? I thought you couldn't trust yourself...

I'd argue that many aspects of Christianity are similar to those of cults. A classic characteristic of cults is that cult leaders claim to have Divine information and knowledge that normal people cannot access, and, due to this, people must accept the preconceived doctrine of such leaders without doubt, or else they may be seen as faithless and/or controlled by "unwanted forces". This produces paranoia, a lack of personal thinking, and a sense of enslavement. People may force themselves to believe that they engage in such harmful behaviors out of pure "love" or "passion". However, people sometimes attach themselves to harmful sources, believing that they are what keep them safe. Certain teachings may justify harmful actions on the teacher's behalf such as *"I understand things that you cannot..."* and by convincing others that their wellbeing –

and in the case of Fundamentalist Christianity – their eternity is in danger.

Feelings of anxiety due to a sense of being endangered are commonly attributed to "the Holy Spirit", causing people to believe that they're under Divine guidance when they are truly ill. Feelings of euphoria during Church performances may also be attributed to "the Holy Spirit", when in truth, these feelings likely emerge from being in high energy spaces in which many people share a similar, uplifting experience. Not to mention, that many other religions have claimed explanations to phenomena that have not been proven factual, suggesting that predominantly religious explanations as to why such events happened are indeed mere intuition or backed by pseudoscience. For example, many myths have claimed to explain the phenomenon known to Christians as

"Noah's Flood". Due to the fact that pieces that were supposedly from Noah's ark were found, Christians may engage in confirmation bias without critical thinking. What if there is another explanation? And for the many other theories and religious explanations as to what those pieces were, wouldn't all these theories be confirmed as well? Why are *you* right?

People may feel uncomfortable exploring these feelings of cognitive dissonance, and may resort to accusing religious characters, such as "the Holy Spirit" of guiding them or supposed demons of deceiving them, a common coping mechanism when faced with contradictory information. Another characteristic of cults is that if people are faced with outside information, disproving the teachings of such a cult, the leader may accuse them of being under outside and/or harmful control, further establishing division and thus disregarding one's humanity.

Not to mention that the Bible doesn't claim to be inerrant. In fact, the Bible contains many historically and scientifically factual errors along with a plethora of logical contradictions that disprove itself, and that are also proven to be false due to actual events that happen. For example, according to the Bible, God tells people not to worry about food and clothes because he promises to provide. But in real life, many faithful people go without food or clothes.

My
Enlightenment

There wasn't one exact moment in
which my life, and everything I understood as
I did, changed forever in one of the least
imaginable ways possible. I've always
considered myself to be a "Christian". My
young naive mind once believed that being a
Christian simply meant to believe in Jesus and
God. I even recall a time period when I
considered any theist a Christian. Since I
wasn't yet touched by the cruelty and
judgment of society, I innocently believed that
everyone had the right to believe their own

thing and in their own way and that it wasn't too big of a problem. I wish my mind would've stayed that child-like, except for diving into the depths of torment in which it did, but I can't cry over spilled milk.

I used to think I was born a "Christian". In my young mind, how couldn't I have been? God was my father and he put me on this Earth, hence I'm a Christian... *right?* Now tell me, what young child would think this way. People often believe what their parents believed, and what *THEIR* parents believed and what **THEIR** parents believed. And one thing about people is that when they believe something, they can see no wrong in their belief. *"Don't question God, you just don't understand...," "Satan is just trying to lead you astray like the sneaky serpent he is...," "I've seen miracles, I can TESTIFY that what I believe is* *true."* All too common statements in response to any sort of critical thinking.

In Christianity, we're taught to distrust ourselves because only God knows and only He is good. We're taught that the Devil prowls like a hungry lion, waiting to deceive you — waiting to lure you from God. This kind of teaching is passed down generation by generation. It's a status quo. Fear is instilled into the minds of the innocent, and once their innocence washes away with their age, they continue to spread these statements. Do they even know where it came from? *"God! It came from God! The Bible said so! The pastor said so! GOD said so!"* Really? REALLY? Has God verbally spoken to you? *"Yes, he has! Through the Bible and in Church!"* Who ever said that God wrote the Bible? People. Are people God? No. *"But, but, but..."* This is how most people react when their traditional beliefs are challenged. They go into hyper-defensive mode because they need to protect their truth. They need to protect their foundation. For if their foundation crumbles, so does the world that they've constructed all around them.

The human mind craves certainty. *"This must be the way! There CAN'T be another way!"* Their mind fights to keep them alive. People don't understand the depths of religious trauma. It penetrates into the deepest parts of the human psyche. It becomes a part of us. The fine line between religious teachings and ourselves are blurred. We blindly believe what we're taught because we're told that by doing so we're practicing blind faith. I'd say that you're just practicing being blind.

Christianity discourages critical thinking and trusting of one's self. It was written and constructed by men for men. "God" didn't make Christianity. God didn't write the Bible. God didn't give us the concept of sin. God didn't tell us there was a Heaven and a hell. The "God" figure made people, and people made things. Blurring the lines between Creator and creation is a dangerous thing.

Fear of hell, sin, evil, and punishment is instilled into pure minds and passed down through each new generation. People demonstrate symptoms of mental illness but believe that they're pleasing God. They're pleasing their own concept of God. You can't convince me in a million years that ONE way is the way. People wrote the Bible based on what people said that they heard other people supposedly say about the disciples' and Jesus' teachings, YEARS after their deaths. It was then translated by the people who killed Jesus OVER AND OVER AND OVER AGAIN. It was manipulated and corrupted by corrupt leaders.

It was translated over and over in many different languages, not to mention the cultural, language, and time gaps that may alter our understanding. It contains metaphors, stories, symbolic teachings, controversial teachings, and most importantly OPINIONS. It was NOT written by any Divine figure. Flaws, opinions, and things that simply just don't apply to us anymore are scattered all throughout the books and chapters of the Bible. The Bible doesn't even claim to be inerrant.

Although some Biblical events have been proven, *so* many others have been *dis*proven. And even if the basis of Biblical events did happen, consider these factors: how could bias or cultural norms of the time play a role in the writing of these biblical texts? Why do we full heartedly believe that their interpretation of events is the only true way? How are we so sure that the recording of their events is true?

Many teachings that may back up theories of the Bible's inerrancy may say things like *"It's called having faith,"* or *"God calls us to rely not on our own understanding."* But the people who created these teachings obviously *wanted* us to believe *their* way. Christianity is not a personal relationship with God, it is a religion. Period. If it were personal, we wouldn't be sinners. We wouldn't be punished or held up to extreme moral standards. We wouldn't all have to believe the same thing. For goodness sake, we wouldn't even be judged with the possibility of burning in *Hell* for eternity if it was purely out of genuine love and personal relationship.

Viewing "God" and how life works based on ancient teachings of imperfect people with imperfect pasts who literally *want* us to believe them, and claiming that these views are from the one and only *God* is extremely problematic. We become delirious and believe that it's the Holy Spirit's influence. We can't even see fault in this. Our world begins to crumble. We begin to question. We begin to compulsively pray. We may think that we lose ourselves, but we're just losing the illusion that we've tied to ourselves.

To tie this back to a point I made earlier, we weren't born into our religion. We were born as *people*, and then we were taught how to see the world. We were discouraged to have a view of our own. Fear was instilled into us in order to coerce us into human and problematic beliefs by people who claim to know the one and only truth of God. We are taught that hate and pride are justifiable because since we are God's true elect and we have the only way, others are all less than.

Now I'm not saying to abandon your beliefs. And there's a possibility that I may be wrong. But I'm just asking you to consider the possibility that you could be wrong too. My views don't have to be yours, but your views don't have to be the views of privileged Western white males who created a religion way too based on homophobia, racism, discrimination, pride, and sexism.

Forcing people to view life in certain ways due to certain stories and judging their actions isn't the will of any Creator. Even Jesus himself was disappointed in the religious institutions. That very disappointment and rebellion is what got him killed. And his murderers did just what he taught against: created a religion. And of course, they made it in his name: Christianity.

You don't need to stop your religion. All I advise is that next time you open up scripture and begin to read, just think. You don't have to think in the way that I do, but just open yourself up to the possibility that maybe even one little thing that you believe may be wrong. And the supposed "uncertainty" that you may feel as a result of doing so may just set you free.

Questioning The Dogma

Testimony: I just don't understand. After struggling with debilitating anxiety and OCD over religious themes, I've come to realize that so many beliefs and concepts of life that I used to hold dearly are so twisted and harmful in nature. Not only are they illogical, but they're dangerous. I don't like to use clinically significant psychological jargon terms loosely, so I'm very mindful when I make these statements. However, I would confidently 100% claim that I was traumatized by religion. All of my days were filled with constant dread, anxiety, headaches, restlessness, agitation, crying, ruminating, regretting, doubting, sulking, and exhausting mental compulsions, just to battle the ways that religion had poisoned my mind. I was brainwashed because I didn't have the chance to think for myself. I was taught that thinking for myself was bad, so I gave into anxiety every day. I gave into a personified, punitive, vengeful, murderous, and tyrannical image of God, and I believed that this image was one of love. I thought that signs of literal mental illness were the Holy Spirit, and I believed that being myself was a terribly sinful and disgusting act. But I'm no longer slaving myself to these thoughts. If I have to continue to believe in a punitive and vengeful God, an odd system of supposed "free will", a twisted version of love, an illogical idea of salvation, and all-together nasty beliefs, then I will just live life very cynical and depressed, praising an image of "God" that I think is so messed up.

Some of my questions and thoughts:

<u>A Loving God?</u>

I don't understand why people call the traditional Western view of "God" one of "love". The theology basically claims that God sent his one and only truly good son to die a brutal death for the sins of wicked people. It proceeds to claim that although we deserve eternal fiery torment due to our ever-so-evil selves, God resurrected His precious Son so that everyone can go to Heaven and worship Him forever. If you were to ask past me how I felt about such theology, I would say that it is the greatest proclamation of love, in fact, it is way better than I could do. However, I simply accepted what people had told me was the greatest act of "love" towards mankind without forming an opinion for myself. So after critically thinking about this theology, I've decided that this is very odd for many reasons. According to traditional Christian views, God created everything, God is also all-powerful, all-seeing, and all-knowing, meaning that if he truly desires something, He has the complete and ultimate power to go forward with his will. However, this claim must mean that God knew that people were going to sin, and He had the power to stop this from happening, but He let it happen. If God's will is ultimate, He must have allowed sin to be placed in the hearts of mankind, yet He felt the need to test their devotion towards Him for some reason. And why would God create people to worship Him? That just doesn't make sense to me. He also could've just solved all the problems that He with His "all-powerful" and "good will" allowed to happen, but he didn't; Instead, this "unconditionally loving" God decided to allow great suffering amongst his "favored creation" and sentenced them to an eternal punishment of agonizing hellfire. Most apologetic Christians defend this logic with the overused statement that "the flesh can't understand the totality of God's plan, but through the revelation of His spirit, you will come to trust Him." However, God also made us to not understand His will. And no one can convince me, no matter what "God's will" may be, that there was NO other way to allow for more peace in the world. If me as an inferior human being that "can't understand the totality of God's plan" can think of a more humane way of solving the problems that this God supposedly allowed, then why can't He?

And the impulse to not question anything due to the threat of being under the Devil's control or God's anger demonstrates an unhealthy relationship with God through toxic fear. And God also has the power to be stronger than the Devil, to make sure that he can't torture people, or to make him cease to exist, but He keeps the Devil there for his mysterious plan that no "dumb" human can possibly seem to understand.

All-Powerful God & World Suffering Coexisting?

There are only two options: *The traditional Western concept of God is not all-powerful and all-knowing* OR *that God is not all-loving.* There just can't be an intelligent and loving God that allows mass violence, world hunger, childhood illness, and such horrible circumstances of the world to exist. Blaming these problems on Satan does not make sense because it just proves the belief that God gave Satan more power than Him, which makes apologetic Christiansrefute their own claims. If God decides to save some people and allow the hurt of others for His mysterious will, then there is a demonstration of favor for some of His children, and not His others. Why would a Father love some of His children over the rest, even allowing for them to die? That doesn't reflect the image painted of an unconditionally loving God. One of these narratives has to give.

Prayer & God's Will Co-existing?

If God has a pre-planned will, then prayer shouldn't be able to work, and vice versa. Prayer would be disturbing God's predestined will, and if "the answer to your prayers is a part of God's will", then your prayers aren't truly being answered, your desires just happen to overlap. When something good happens after prayer, some people may claim it is a testament of God's goodness, but as soon as there's catastrophe, they claim it to be "God's will". Do they even know what they believe?

Other Religions & Diversity

Why would God allow for the beauty of diversity and other worldviews just to punish those who don't find the one "correct" way? So many people are filled with love, light, and kindness and they walk in ways much more admirable than most supposed "Christians". I can argue that a lot of Christians are some of the world's most terrible people. There was love and joy and "signs of afterlife" before Christianity, so how can it be the only way? If the Devil/enemy spirits are deceiving them, why can't God just help? (Referring to my past takes on the problem of just responding with "God's will") And if God really wanted everybody to be saved, why would he allow such an urgent message to become distorted? According to this logic, God allowed people to blindly walk into their own doom, having the power to help, but deciding to give them "free will" by either forcing them to love Him or by threatening Hell or sending them to Hell. So free, isn't it?